Tangible
press

LESSONS

BASS LINES, SESSIONS and ON THE ROAD STORIES
by
HARVEY BROOKS

LESSONS
BASS LINES, SESSIONS and ON THE ROAD STORIES

© 2025 by Harvey Brooks

All rights reserved. No part of this publication may be reproduced, distributed, stored in a retrieval system, or transmitted in any form or by any means, electronic, mechanical, photocopying, recording, or otherwise, without prior written permission of the publisher, except in the case of brief quotations embodied in a book review. For information regarding permission requests, write to the publisher, Tangible Press, addressed "Attention: Permissions Coordinator," at www.tangiblepress.net

Tangible Press is a wholly owned and operated
Subdivision of Punk Hart Productions LLC

Cover design by John Howells

Printed in the United States of America
First Printing, 2025

ISBN: 1-7375810-4-3
ISBN-13: 978-1-7375810-4-8

Dedicated to the one I love, best friend, wife, and partner Bonnie Behar Brooks.

INTRODUCTION

Playing Electric Bass Guitar

If you are looking at this book because you are familiar with my style of playing or if one of your parents turned you on to me, whatever the circumstance, I'm glad you are here.

I have been privileged to play on many classic albums throughout my career by being at the right place at the right time. For me, the right place was playing bass on Bob Dylan's Highway 61 Revisited album (1965). Buddy Al Kooper got me the session as a payback for a gig I got him at the 1964 World's Fair. Thanks Al! The right time is when you acquire a bass guitar and begin bass lessons or join your first band and start learning the bass lines and chords of songs you like and then begin to create your own music.

Recording and performing with Pop & Jazz artists such as Miles Davis, Bob Dylan, The Doors, Jimi Hendrix, Seals & Croft and folk artists Fred Neil, Eric Andersen at Vanguard Records, Richie Havens, Karen Dalton, Cass Elliot, Peter, Paul and Mary, Tom Rush, David Blue, John Sebastian, Jim & Jean, and Ian and Sylvia and joining up to tour with The Doors, Bob Dylan, Mike Bloomfield (Electric Flag) Paul Butterfield's Blues Band, Donald Fagen's (Steely Dan) Rock & Soul Review, Al Kooper and Clarence Clemons Red Bank Rockers (Bruce Springsteen Band) was the payoff for the time I spent practicing, playing in garages, local bars, coffee houses and learning how, what and when to play on Rhythm and Blues gigs.

I am talking to you as one bass player to another. There are many possible reasons and events in your life that directed you to the electric bass. I suggest these three lead the list. Love, Music and money. All three of these factors when performed in this order promise a rewarding lifestyle. The bass player provides direction and comfort in his bassline's choice of notes.

Bass is the bottom, that's where music starts its journey through a song. The bass note is usually the bottom note of a chord. It is the rhythmic heartbeat. The chord is made up of three or more notes stacked up on top of each other. The bass line winds its way through the music with notes jumping on and off, changing the sound of the chords.

Chapter One

THE ELECTRIC BASS

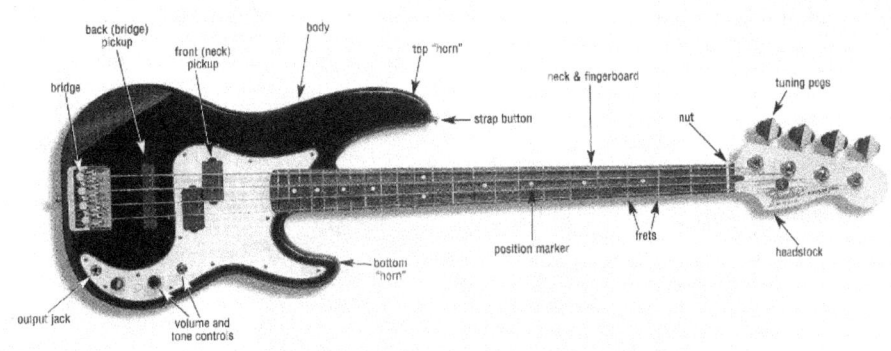

Your Bass

The only requirement for your bass is that it's not too heavy on your shoulders and neck and that the strings are not too high from the finger board making it difficult to press down which can lead to frustration and the "not want to play because it hurts" syndrome. I advise going to a music store in your neighborhood and try playing some of the electric basses. Even if you want to buy online and you've never played a bass before, you will get different feelings from different basses. You want to be able to press the strings down easily. There are many basses that are reasonably priced to fit your budget. My first bass was a Tower bass that was made in Japan. A single pickup with one volume and one tone control knob.

My next bass was a Rickenbacker. It was my first encounter with two pickups and the world of different tones for different tunes. Now I could adjust the sound of the pickups to fit into the musical mix. The pickup closest to the neck or fingerboard adds a deeper bass tone and the pickup closest to the bridge adds a sharper or treble sound. Each pickup has a volume and separate tone control.

The picture here is my 1978 Fender precision bass. I replaced the original precision pickups with an EMG PJ setup and added a Hip Shot Bass D tuner which lowers the E string one whole tone down to a D. The original neck was replaced after an accident. The new neck is an "A" neck, just a little bigger than a Fender jazz neck.

My stage rig for concerts is the amplifier sitting behind my bass, the Hartke LH1000 Bass amp with a 410 XL Bass Cabinet.

EMG PJ setup

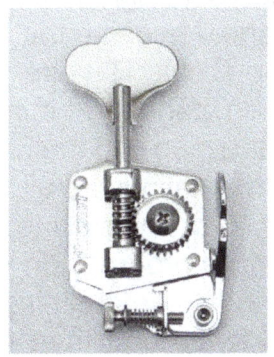

Hip Shot Bass D tuner

As a result of hanging out at the Café Au Go Go on Bleeker Street in Greenwich Village, I became the house bassist playing many spontaneous sets with artists like Richie Havens, Jimi Hendrix and Fred Neil, meeting them for the first time on stage. Sometimes I knew the song but most times I didn't. I would walk up and plug into the provided bass amp and say "what key", knowing that knowing the key would allow me to use the basic and most fitting notes from the scale. Usually sticking to the first and fifth note of each chord. After learning the chord progression via repetition of the verses and choruses we were performing and determining the theme licks, theme licks are licks played more than two times and then connecting the spaces around the melody of the singer or instrumentalist.

The bass in the picture above is an Epiphone EB-2, which I used to play with folk artists such as Tim Hardin and Rambling Jack Elliot at the Newport Folk Festival. This bass has a "Baritone" switch for additional sound-color. It gave a warm round sound that supported these artists as an upright acoustic bass would.

Long Horn Bass

I remember many days hanging out with bass and guitar designer Dan Armstrong at his downstairs Greenwich Village shop on La Guardia off Bleeker St. talking bass and bass pickups with Dan and pickup master Bill Lawrence. The last time I was there many years ago, I bought two basses from Dan to take on tour that would fit into one case. As Dan was intonating the Long Horn, this weird guy came running down the stairs. The King of shock rock Alice Cooper made his entrance. All kinds of folk could be found at Dan Armstrong's shop.

First made in 1958, this punchy short scale bass is heard on countless recordings.

- 1958 longhorn bass body shape
- 29.75" short-scale neck
- Number of frets: 24
- Traditional bridge with single rosewood saddle
- 2 high output, high impedance lipstick® pickups
- 2 stacked volume/tone control sets

Dan Armstrong Strong Six String bass

I used both basses on my gig with folksingers Jim & Jean on a winter tour though United States and Canada. One of the concerts was in the city of Orillia at a hockey rink. The audience was seated on a gigantic black tarp that was lying atop the ice playing field. It was so cold I had to cut the fingertips off my gloves. I used the six-string bass for melodic songs and the Long Horn for more of an upright bass feel. I was able to fit both basses into one case which made the backseat I was sitting in much more comfortable.

BASS AMPLIFIER

You also need a practice amp. Bass practice amps are small and should have a headphone jack so you can practice without disturbing family members or your pet dog or cat. Hartke, Ampeg and Fender are examples of brand names that are available.

Below a Hartke practice amp and on the right is my current setup of Hartke LH1000 amp and XL 4-10. When using a patch chord or cable to connect from the output of the bass to the input of the amp make sure the amp's volume knob is turned off.

On the left is the 1964-66 Fender Dual Showman I used for all the Electric Flag and Super session recordings at Columbia recording studio in Hollywood California.

Pictured on the right is the Ampeg B-15 that I used on most of my recording sessions and gigs in the 1960's and 70's.

The tone controls should be set "flat" or at 12 0'clock. Turn on the power and slowly adjust the volume to an appropriate level. Be careful, too much volume could blow out the speaker.

TUNING

Plug your bass cable into an amplifier input and tune it up with an easily available mobile phone app such as Guitar Tuna. To start tuning you set the tuner by selecting four, five or six string bass and then you're then ready to tune up. If you notice that the string you are tuning is sharp in pitch, tune down below the target pitch and slowly tighten the string until it's up to pitch and in tune.

Tuning your amplifier sound is next. By experimenting with the bass, mid, and treble equalizer (EQ) knobs you can become familiar with the different sounds as you add or subtract the EQ, always playing to hear how your sound is affected. When I arrive at the gig and start to set up on stage for the soundcheck I will usually set up on the floor of the stage and tweak the EQ's, bass, mid and treble to make the room sound good.

Your sound comes from a combination of the amp's equalization, your right-hand plucking technic and your left hand's fingering strength. So much of your sound is created by the way you press the strings into the neck. I press the strings using my fingertip to get control of the string.

The question is, how do you get your bass to sound like all those bass players that you love. Answer, keep practicing and keep playing!!!

Chapter Two

PLAYING POSITIONS

STANDING
- Buy a comfortable strap between 2 and a half and three inches wide. Leather or woven cotton are good choices. A padded, stretchy neoprene strap will help absorb the weight of the instrument.

- Adjust the straps so that both hands can be comfortable on the bass. With your left hand at your side, bend the elbow, bringing your forearm up. This is your optimal position for the left hand.

- Hold your right arm straight in front of you at shoulder height, and let the hand hang down naturally. Bend your elbow and bring your arm in towards your body. That is the optimal position for your right hand.

- Be sure to avoid any extreme bends in either wrist.

- Run the guitar cable under your strap to avoid pulling it out of the jack while standing.

SITTING
- It's best to use a strap while sitting to keep the instrument at the proper height.

- Without a strap, rest the bass on your right leg. It may help to use a small footstool under your right foot.

- Keep your left arm off your leg.

- Balance the bass so you don't have to grip the neck, allowing your fingers the freedom to move across the neck freely.

- Angle the neck slightly away from the bass.

LEFT-HAND TECHNIQUE

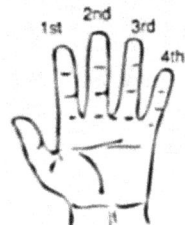

There are two fingering systems.
1-2-4   FINGERING SYSTEM - For the upright and bass guitar.
1-2-3-4 FINGERING SYSTEM - For bass guitar only.

The fingers are numbered 1 through 4.
I use the 1-2-3-4 system. This fingering requires a little more effort because the lower frets are farther apart. Start with the pad of your thumb in the middle of the neck, make sure it doesn't stick over the top.

The thumb is positioned between the first and second fingers.
- Place your first finger directly behind the 1st fret of the E string, pressing down lightly.
- Place your second finger on the 2nd fret.
- Place your third finger on the 3rd fret.
- Place your fourth finger on the 4th fret.
-

Notice that we have access to four frets—this is called a position. The position is determined by the fret the index finger is on. First position 1st fret, second position 2nd fret, etc.

The next thing to do is to learn the notes on the finger board and at the same time, use this exercise to build up finger strength. As you press down on each string say the note names. Ex 1: E string, Open E, F, F#, G, G# and the next string Open A…etc. Try to play all notes with your left-hand fingertips.

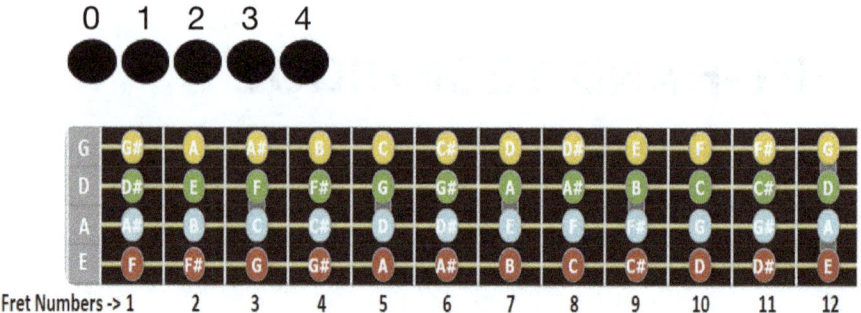

Fingers...... Play 0 (open string), fret and finger are the same for each string starting with the fourth string open E, then Third A, Second D & First

RIGHT-HAND TECHNIQUE

FINGER STYLE
The most common approach for playing the electric bass is fingerstyle — — ex. Using the index and middle fingers of the right hand to play the strings. The fingers give you a warm full sound that can be controlled easily by developing touch sensitivity.

- Let your fingers hang comfortably over the strings; don't curl them.
- Start by resting the tip of the thumb gently on the pickup.
- Using the fleshy pad of your finger, place it on top of the string.

E STRING
Gently push down and across the top of the E string, letting your finger come to rest against the pad of your thumb. Alternate strokes between the index and middle fingers. Repeat this until you feel comfortable. Play lightly; too much force will give you a distorted sound.

A STRING
Move your finger to the A String. Push down and across the string, letting your finger come to rest against the E string at the end of the stroke. Alternate fingers; repeat several times.

D STRING
Drop your thumb to the E string. Move your finger to the D string, push down and across, letting your finger come to rest against the A string. Alternate fingers and repeat.

G STRING
Drop your thumb onto the A string, and make it lean against the E string. This mutes both strings to prevent unwanted ringing. Put your index finger on the G string. Push down and across the string, letting your finger come down to rest against the D string. Alternate fingers and repeat.

TIP: As you alternate fingers, place each finger down for the next stroke just slightly ahead of time to mute the previous note. This will give you a more controlled sound.

Chapter Three

Bass Strings

This photo was taken at The Golden Bear in Huntington Beach on the eve of our first record release. The band had a ten-day engagement there. After the first night's show at four o'clock in the morning while listening to reel-to-reel tapes of the show that night, police knocked at the door and guitarist Michael Bloomfield answered the knock and cracked the door open telling the police they needed a warrant to enter the room. The officer stuck a gun through the cracked opening and said this is my warrant. "I smell marijuana" The cops came in and searched the room going through the instrument cases, suitcases, and the instruments finding some heroin and a small amount of reefer. The next morning our manager Albert Grossman sent his L.A. lawyer to bail us out.

At the time of this Electric Flag ad, I was playing a Fender Jazz bass with La Bella 0760M flat wounds. I still play La Bella strings today using 760FL Medium Gauge .043, .060, .080, .104 and 7760 FX Light gauge .039, .056, .077, .096 depending on what a song calls for feel-wise. I use the medium gauge for the singer/songwriter style and lighter gauge for melodic stylings.

How to Change Bass Guitar Strings

Detune and remove

You'll start by removing the old strings. This the easiest part. Cut them one-at-a-time after detuning the string all the way down before doing so. This allows the neck to relax and better adjust to the tension change. You don't absolutely have to cut them, but we do because they're easier to remove. Old strings aren't typically reused, but they can be repurposed or recycled.

1. Detune the string until it no longer produces a pitch.
2. Use wire cutters to cut it near the pickup(s) region.
3. Remove from the tuning post and bridge.

Install new strings!

Now that the old strings are out, let's put the new ones on. The most important tip when installing new strings is to not overtighten them too much too soon. That's because the strings are stretching and need to adjust to the new tension. You should be able to install the new strings and bring them up to pitch, but they'll need to be retuned a few times until they stabilize. Just be cautious that if tuned up too high *(above standard tuning)*, the strings could be too stressed and snap. To prevent breaking, change each string one at a time, paying attention to which one you're replacing, and which tuner key is used to tighten it.

Identify and insert

1. Remove the strings from their packaging and uncoil them. Identify each string by either the packaging label or by the color of its ball end.
2. Insert the string through its corresponding bridge entry. Carefully pull it all the way through, using your finger to prevent it from grinding against the bridge hole. Align the string over both its bridge saddle and nut guides.

Crimp and trim

1. Leaving no slack, guide the string from the nut to the center of its tuning post. Measure an additional 2 – 3" of string from the tuning post, and then bend (aka crimp) the string at a 90° angle.
2. Measure an additional ½" – 1" of string from the crimp and trim it off with the wire cutters.
3. Only the silk portion of the string should wrap around the tuning post or else the string will break.

Stretch and tune

Once restrung, you'll notice that the strings will keep going out of tune. That's because they need to adapt to the new tension. One way to decrease the time it takes for the strings to adapt is by stretching them. Perform a stretching motion along the entire length of the string to acclimate it quicker and stabilize the pitch. Tune, stretch, repeat.

1. Using a tuner, bring the string up to pitch.
2. Lightly stretch the string along its length (the fretboard).
3. Repeat the tuning and stretching cycle until each string's pitch stabilizes.

Keeping your bass in tune

Use a minimum number of neat winds around the tuner post. A few wraps around the tuner post will usually work for wound strings, more may be required for unwound strings. As a guideline, strings with a smaller diameter require more wraps. The goal is to have each wrap neatly stacked, working downward from the tuning peg hole.

Stretch your strings well

Once your new strings are installed and up to pitch, gently tug 8-10 times at various places along the length of the string. Then, push down gently on the string behind the nut and on or behind the bridge to help it seat properly. Now bring it back to pitch.

Repeat this process for each string, as many times as necessary, until the strings begin to stay in tune. Properly stretched strings tend to stay in tune better over their lifespan.

Make Sure Your Bass is Properly Set Up

A good set up will help with many aspects of tuning. For example, uneven frets or an improperly adjusted neck can cause intonation problems. When turning the tuners, strings can hang up at the nut or bridge if the slots aren't cut correctly, causing the pitch of the string to "stick," then jump suddenly. Another crucial element is correct bridge and saddle adjustment because that's where the intonation for the entire bass is set. A good set up is important to playing in tune. If you don't feel comfortable doing a set up yourself, have a professional guitar repairman set up your instrument. It will play, sound, and stay in tune much better with a pro set up.

Tune "Up" to Pitch

Using the tuning keys, start with the string below the target pitch and slowly tighten the string until it is in tune. If you tune a string tighter than it needs to be and go higher than the target pitch, when you tune back down to the correct pitch you can create slack in the string. Not only will this make it harder for the string to settle into the correct tension (pitch) but it will also make it easier to knock the string out of tune as you play. If you notice that the string you are tuning is sharp in pitch, tune down below the target pitch and slowly tighten the string until it's up to pitch and in tune.

Of course, the essential accessory for staying in tune is a tuner. Tuners are simple to use, accurate, and come in many formats: clip-on, stomp box, desktop, etc. A wide variety of types of tuners are available; choose the one that suits you and use it often — it's not uncommon for a bassist to tune between each song onstage and in the studio, between each take. The number one thing you can do to improve your sound is to play in tune!

How to Set Your Intonation

Using an electronic tuner, tune all the open strings to their correct pitches. Starting with your lowest string, fret the string at the 12th fret. Make sure you press the string straight down. You want this fretted note to be in tune. It should be the same note as the open string.

Check the electronic bass tuner to see if you are flat (too low) or sharp (too high). If you are flat, you need to shorten the string by moving the saddle forward. If you are sharp, you need to add length to the string by moving the saddle backward. After you adjust the saddle, double check that the open string is still in tune.

Do the same for each string. You will discover that it is impossible to get every single fret perfectly in tune. This is normal. Fretted instruments have a natural flaw where they can't be perfectly intonated. You can just get really close. If you're interested in why, look up "equal temperament" or "just intonation" in a music dictionary.

Learning Basic Scales

Now that you have started to play your bass that is in tune, and has a nice warm mellow sound, what's next? For the bassist who has no previous experience we start off playing a very friendly C scale.

Example: The first finger, when placed on the first fret, is in the first position. When the first finger is placed on the second fret, you are in second position

A fretted electric bass should play the notes directly behind the fret. Each fret is a one-half step. The positions are numbered according to what fret the first finger is placed on.

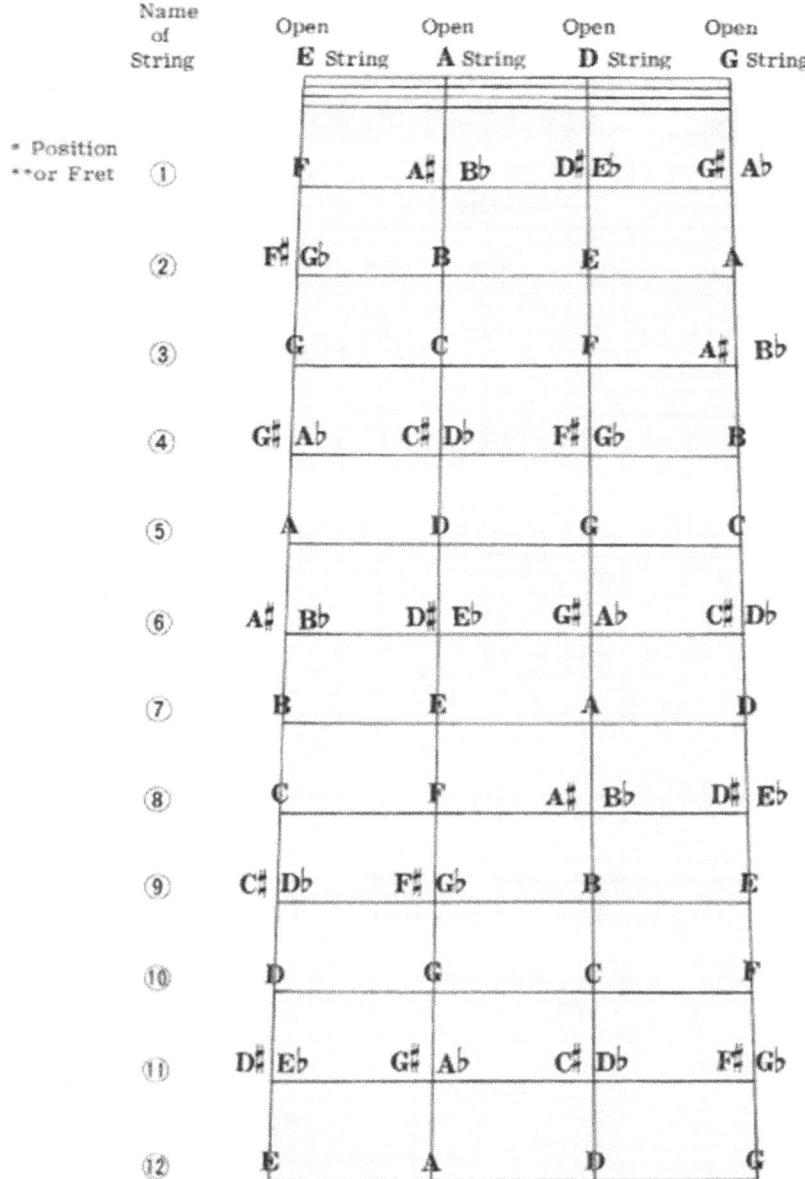

Next page is an explanation and recommended finger positioning on each fret.

C Major Scale Fingerings

Universal Fingering

Open Position

Extension Fingering

One String Fingering
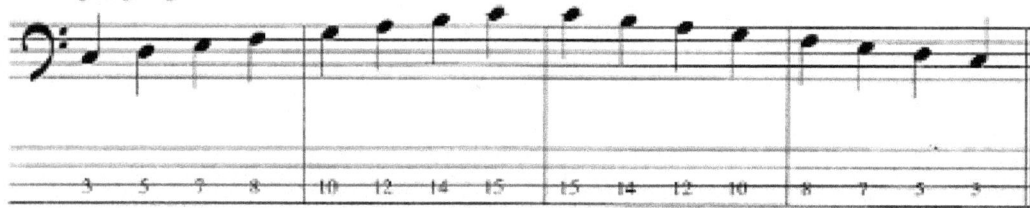

Cmajor #1 Most Efficient Route

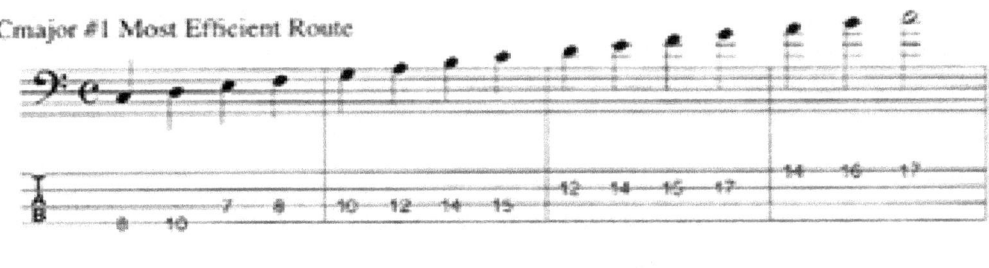

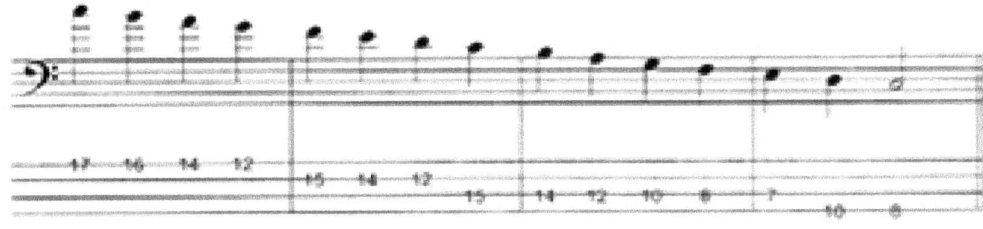

Cmajor #2 From "Home Position"

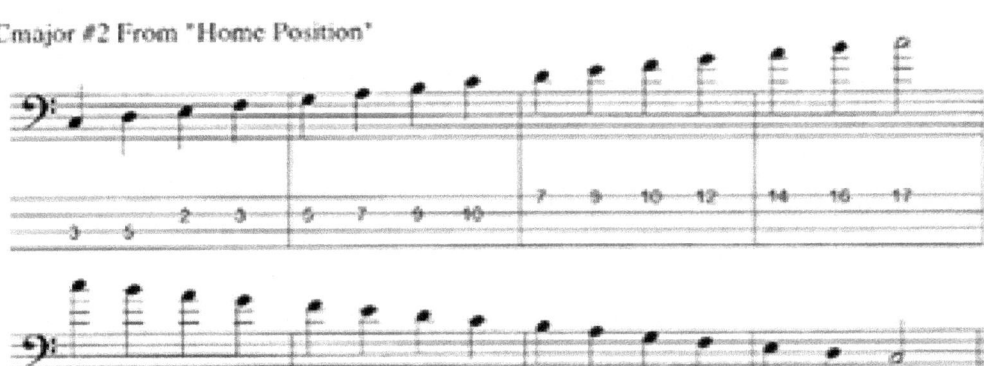

Cmajor# 3 Extension Fingering, use pivot between fingers 2-3

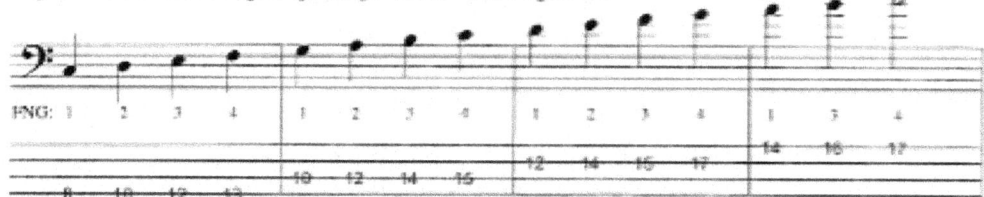

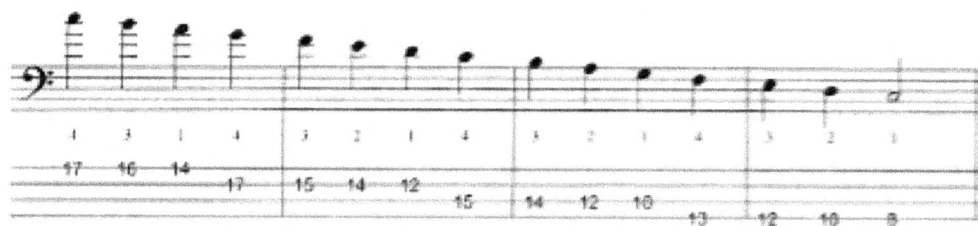

Using Open Strings as a "Bounce Point" for Shifting

F major w/ bounce

Chapter Four

Chord Charts

I learned how to read chord charts on the gig. There were no rehearsals most of the time. As a freelance musician playing with different groups, I listened to the drummer for the rhythm pattern and keyboard or rhythm guitar for the chords and unison lines. First and foremost, I listened to the vocalist or instrumental melody to leave space for the words Some bandleaders provided me with recordings of the tunes so I could hear what the original bassline was. The first thing I had to do was find the root or tone center of the music. It's a single pitch by which the notes are organized. Think of it as the center of gravity. It's a magnetic force to which all other pitches in the song are attracted. You can throw them in any direction you like, but they will always return to the tonal center.

Developing your musical ear to find and play the root or tonal center puts you inside the song and teaches you how to follow a chord progression.

A chord progression (or just "progression") is a sequence of chords harmonized and played in succession. It is the road map that directs you from the beginning of the song until you arrive at the end. For example, the bass line of Jimi Hendrix's *Little Wing*, consisting of the Root Note of each chord in the song, looks like this:

Key of G
Vi   I   ii   vi   iii   ii   IV   I   bVII IV
Em /// I G /// I Am /// I Em /// I Bm /// I Am / C / I G / F / I C / I
V   V   VI IV   V   V
D /// I D / E C I D/// I D /// I - Key of G

The above chord progression has Roman Numerals as well as letters to identify chord forms. I have been on a gig, at a session or playing the third or fourth set on a bar gig when the lead singer says I can't make the high notes and says let's lower the key. Jimi's version of Little Wing is in "G". Taking the song a whole step down into the key of "F" goes like this:

Key of F

| Vi | I | ii | Vi | iii | ii | IV | I | bVII | IV |

Dm /// I F /// I Gm /// I Dm /// I Am /// I Gm / Bb/ I F/ I Eb / I Bb / I

| V | V | VI IV | V | V |

C /// I C / D Bb I C/// I C /// I - Key of F

What is a Key - and how does it work

A key is a series of seven tones arranged in an alpha-numerical order. Together they make up a major scale, KEY.

Major scale formula W W H W W W H.   W=Whole step, H=Half step
Minor scale formula W H W W W H W

Different types of numbers are used to describe the notes in a key.

The following example is in the key of C Major. The same formula applies to all Major keys.

Letters	C	D	E	F	G	A	B	C
Degrees	1	2	3	4	5	6	7	1
Chords	I	ii	iii	IV	V7	VI	Vii	I
	M	m	m	M	M	m	m7b5	M
Solfegge.	Do	Re	Mi	Fa	Sol	La	Ti	Do

Nashville Number System
And Transposition Chart

1	2	3	4	5	6	7	1
C	D	E	F	**G**	A	B	C
G	A	B	C	**D**	E	F#	G
D	E	F#	G	**A**	B	C#	D
A	B	C#	D	**E**	F#	G#	A
E	F#	G#	A	**B**	C#	D#	E
B	C#	D#	E	**F#**	G#	A#	B
F#	G#	A#	B	**C#**	D#	E#	F#
C#	D#	E#	F#	**G#**	A#	B#	C#
F	G	A	**Bb**	C	D	E	F
Bb	C	D	**Eb**	F	G	A	Bb
Eb	F	G	**Ab**	Bb	C	D	Eb
Ab	Bb	C	**Db**	Eb	F	G	Ab
Db	Eb	F	**Gb**	Ab	Bb	C	DB
Gb	Ab	Bb	**Cb**	Db	Eb	F	Gb

Most Common Chord Types

Major	Minor	Minor	Major	Major	Minor	Dim	
I	ii	iii	IV	V	vi	vii°	I

Most Common Exceptions

	2maj	3maj	4min	5min	6maj	7maj	
		b3				b7	
				#5			
#1°			#4°				

The Nashville Number System is a quick and easy way to write chord charts to songs in a way that others (well, others who are familiar with the system) can easily read. One of the main benefits is that it works regardless of the key of the song, and it clearly shows the song's structure

Chapter Five

Capitalizing on opportunities

I started out on my musical journey by learning two chords on the guitar that led to my first gig earning fifty cents. I asked my parents if I got a job and bought a guitar would they pay for guitar lessons. They said yes! My friend, Bob Rose, who taught me the two chords and hired me for my first gig also invited me to join his new band. The band The Citations had two guitars, saxophone, and drums. We would play Synagogue and church dances. In my last year of high school, we were connected to a young New York politician who became the band's manager. After hearing Monk Montgomery play the electric bass with Lionel Hampton's band at one of his political events, he said that our band needs an electric bass and that we only needed one guitar. That was the beginning of my life as a bass player.

In addition to the Citations, I started playing gigs with Queens NYC friend Al Kooper's band the Aristocrats after his bass player left the band to go to dental school. So now I was in two bands. I was starting to play pickup gigs as well and had to learn the hit tunes of the day on my own since there were no rehearsals most of the time. There were R&B, Beatles, Rolling Stones, and top 10 tunes. This was my music school. Eventually I got gigs in the show and dance clubs in Greenwich Village and began networking with musicians and artist managers. This led to working with Bang recording artist Freddie Scott whose manager Carmine "Wassel" DeNoia also managed the vocal group The Exciters. They were promoting their top forty hit *Tell Him* and would be going out on tour and needed a bass player. Carmine suggested this would be a good thing for me to do. This was my first road tour, and I was eighteen years old.

One opportunity taken advantage of leads to others. My parents were very supportive, and Pop would let me drive the family car to my gigs. Playing four to six nights a week with different bands taught me the musical vocabulary that would eventually lead me to Bob Dylan.

For the next three years I played gigs throughout the Five Boroughs of New York City. While playing a five night a week gig at the Sniffen Court Inn on Thirty-sixth Street and Third Avenue in Manhattan I got a call from Al Kooper inviting me to play on Dylan's *Highway 61* Album.

Dylan's *Highway 61 Revisited* album was my first opportunity in the world of pop music. I was coming into the session as a replacement for the bass chair that wasn't being filled to Bob Dylan's satisfaction. I was able to give the music a comfortable feel that helped the overall appeal to Dylan and the new Dylan fans. My job, whether I knew it or not, was to invisibly be there and fill the bottom so Bob wouldn't have to think about it anymore. Al Kooper called me for the session because we had worked together in other situations and knew I would fit.

At the *Highway 61 Revisited* session I met guitarist Mike Bloomfield. We hit it off. Playing on the Dylan sessions created many opportunities, and it was up to me to answer the calls and make the most out of each one of them. Because of the notoriety that playing with Dylan gave me I was hired to play folk album sessions and began jamming anywhere musicians were hanging out. It was at one of these hangouts that Bloomfield asked me to join his new band and move out to Mill Valley, California where the band would be based. First named "American Music Band" and then becoming "The Electric Flag" named after finding an air driven Electric Flag at a local gig in Mill Valley. The electric flag consisted of a three-foot-long pipe with holes drilled into it about three inches apart, a small six-inch base housing a motor large enough to blow some air through the holes and unfurl the *Electric Flag*'s glory that was perched atop the B3 organ's Leslie speaker cabinet located on the right side of the stage.

When opportunity knocks, you got to answer the door!

Chapter Six

To Pick or Not to Pick

The first electric bass I ever saw and heard was a Fender Precision bass being played by the bass player from a local Greenwich Village band called "The Four Saints". He played finger style. So, do I. The rule is that all styles are techniques that you use to create and facilitate what makes the song work best. It is best to practice all the techniques and use what fits the song. It can be more than one technique. The verse can be finger style, the chorus with a pick.

Tone

Playing with a pick gives you a more percussive sound than finger style. It has a sharper and more defined attack than your fingers, and it also opens some options regarding articulation. For example, a pick will make it much easier to do things like down-picking and palm muting simultaneously, giving you a tighter, precise, and percussive sound that can be more difficult to achieve with a finger style technique. These types of benefits can help some bass players stand out in the mix more too.

Of course, the EQ and volume settings will matter the most in a mix, but the brightness and clarity of the pick attack can make the notes pop up more, particularly when you're behind a wall of heavily distorted guitars.

For this reason, learning to play with a pick can be useful for the recording process, especially for metal music. I always record two tracks. One track direct and flat and the other a mic on your favorite bass amp.

Speed

Fast playing isn't everything, but who isn't looking to improve their speed and technique? Doing so only opens more doors to what you can play, and a pick can undoubtedly help with this. Certain speeds are only attainable with a pick. For example, tremolo picking 16th notes at 200 bpm with your fingers with good volume and definition is unreal. To get super-fast with finger style, you must play with a very light touch, and unfortunately, this can cause players to sacrifice volume and dynamics for the sake of speed. There's no point in being fast if the notes aren't being heard clearly.

Increasing tempo with a pick does take practice with a metronome to develop technical efficiency. Picks also tend to be less tiresome for many people if you're applying the appropriate amount of tension in your hands. Additionally, you'll be able to play for more extended periods.

Even though It is totally possible to get ultra-fast playing with the finger style technique, and there are plenty of virtuosic players out there who do it, like Felipe Andreoli, Alex Webster, John Myung, Steve Harris, and Billy Sheehan, most people will be able to reach these speeds significantly easier with a pick.

Versatility

If you're a finger style bass player like me, a pick is just another tool in your arsenal. Just like the slap technique, you don't have to learn it, but would it be helpful? Most likely. Having different techniques at your disposal allows you to be more flexible with what you play and figure out what sounds good to you and suits the song best. Certain songs sound better with a pick and others with fingers, and a lot of great music was created with both techniques over the years and continues to be so. If you're normally a player who uses your fingers, ignoring the use of a pick because you or others think it's cheating is just limiting your options.

Conversely, if you're a guitarist who has transitioned to bass recently and you're unsure if you should stick with the pick, I recommend that you take the time to build up the calluses on your right-hand fingers one & two and left-hand fingertips one two three and four to explore the jazz and R&B punchier fingerstyles.

If you prefer one style over the other and play with that one more, that's fine, but it's a good idea to be proficient with different techniques because you never know when you'll need them. It's never a bad thing to become a more diverse and well-rounded player.

Before and After Gig 10 Worst Fuckups

10. Have wrong start time of gig.
09. Late for the gig, leave home without bass.
08. Break a string with no spare set in the case and must play gig without the fourth string!
07. Forget charts you spent hours working on.
06. Lose address of gig & don't have phone number.
05. Lose parking ticket!
04. Leave car keys with friend who already left the gig.
03. Trip over bass propped up against amp and snap the neck.
02. Must start next gig the same time you finish first gig because of unexpected overtime.
01. Driving off forgetting to pack new bass left on the top of car while packing bass amp.

Most of these fuckups were connected to the smoking of a variety of different geographically grown plants with varying degrees of potency that are now named cannabis.

Don't smoke weed!!! It makes your playing sloppy, your memory almost non-existent, your reflexes slow and turns your lungs into charcoal. If that's OK for you, what do I know?

Seriously, these kinds of behaviors can be avoided by staying relaxed in the natural excitement that accompanies the enjoyment of playing music.

The night before the gig, check for extra string sets, cables, charts, batteries, tuner and tools. You need a wire cutter, string winder, bridge adjustment tool to adjust a movable metal piece called the saddle. Each saddle piece has a groove in the middle of it for its string. It is connected to the bridge base with screws that can be used to adjust its position and height. Different brand bass guitars use different tools to raise and lower and move the saddles forward and backward on the bridge. The last thing I do is go over any charts or recordings of the music, if available.

Chapter Seven

Bass lines

Bob Dylan – *Ballad Of A Thin Man*:

Dylan walked into the studio and started playing the piano. I had never heard the song before, so I started to play along finding the key, chords and rhythm figures. My bass part was based on Dylan's vocal and piano part that he was playing and singing, as well as Al Kooper's spooky organ riffs. As we started to play, Bloomfield's tremolo effected telecaster guitar started to blend in with Kooper's eerie organ sound and Dylan's lyric and vocal started to take over our concentration. The take was not the best one for the band but as an overall performance it was a masterful vocal performance by Dylan….

When we played Forest Hills Tennis Stadium to promote the new *Highway 61 Revisited* album, I found myself standing on stage behind Dylan playing (Bass line below) the tune *Ballad of a Thin Man* with Robby Robertson on guitar instead of Mike Bloomfield and Levon Helm on drums instead of Bobby Gregg. Everything sounded different than in the comfort of the studio. The monitors provided to hear each other's parts on stage were primitive. The fact that we had two weeks of rehearsals to get comfortable with playing Dylan's new tunes added the necessary confidence to make his show work.

Bassline: Ballad of a Thin Man

Ballad of a Thin Man

Bob Dylan

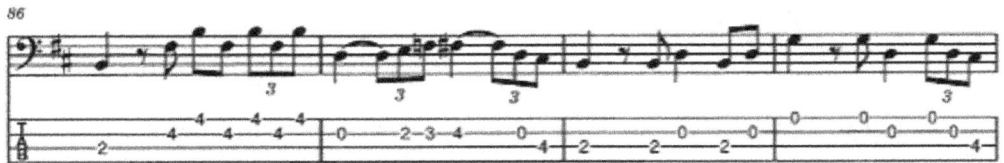
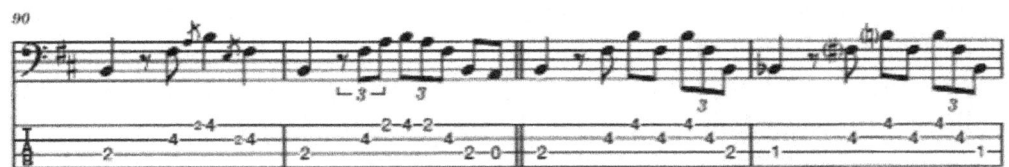

The Doors

Robbie Krieger – I met Robbie backstage after an Electric Flag concert at the Cheetah Club in Venice CA. After some conversation and good weed, he invited me out to his house in Malibu to jam with his band The Doors. Robbie picked me up at the Landmark Hotel where the Flag was staying and set out to Malibu beach where I met keyboardist Ray Manzarek and John Densmore, the Doors drummer. Densmore is a finesse drummer who plays intellectually and solidly. We hit it off immediately. The same with Ray Manzarek who graciously kept his left hand to himself and let me play my own basslines. Robbie and Jim Morrison were the main writers in the group. Robbie is a disciplined player making it easy for me as a bassist to create a bassline to fit the chord progression and rhythm guitar pattern. We had been jamming for a couple of hours when Robbie got a phone call from Jim Morrison wanting us to meet him at the beach.

Jim Morrison – As I said in my book "View from the Bottom," the first thing that Jim said turned out to be an apology about his sloppy bad behavior at the Cheetah Club Electric Flag gig the night before, where he was incoherently rolling around at my feet on stage. We then had this hour-long conversation talking about music, art and creativity. What I didn't know was that I had just auditioned for The Doors' *Soft Parade* album and got the gig.

I first heard about Jim Morrison through his girlfriend Pam, whom I'd met at a Greenwich Village music bar named the Eighth Wonder. I was the bass player in the band, and she worked there as a dancer. We were on a break, and she showed me this Doors poster and told me that this guy Jim Morrison was the lead singer and that she was in love, and he was going to take her to Los Angeles. The next time I saw her was three years later at the Doors *Soft Parade* sessions….

Bassline: Touch Me

Touch Me
The Doors

Standard tuning
♩ = 110

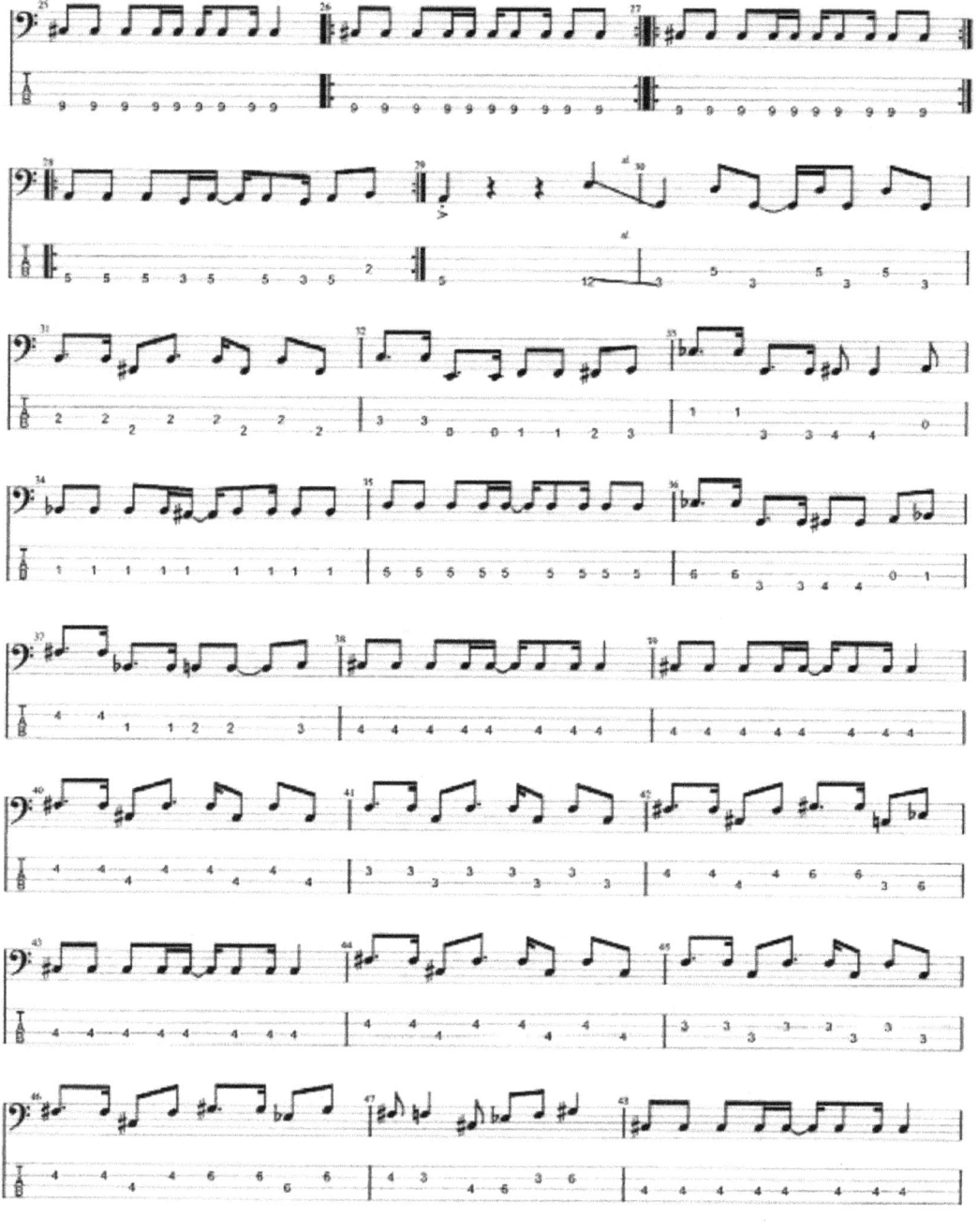

Miles Davis —*Bitches Brew* —

So, I walk into the studio. As I unpack my bass and start to set up Miles waves me over to the back of the studio and says to me "Bass player, when I point to you, you play, when I point and wave, stop. Don't play what you think, play what you hear and feel, and stay on the bottom!"

I understand Miles a lot more now than I did at the Bitches Brew sessions. I was more of a fan back then, being familiar with his recordings which I collected. There was nothing in those recordings to lead me into the freedom spaceship that I stepped into. My role as I understood it was to crawl around the bottom of the music, always setting up humps and bumps in the rhythm with one eye on Miles…. Freedom!

Upright bassist Dave Holland and I were set up next to each other. I told Dave about the conversation between Miles and myself. That was when Dave suggested the electric bass holding the bottom groove and his acoustic bass playing free melodic figures sometimes doubling my bassline. One of the reasons I got the session with Miles was because I played bass on a session called Electric Black Man by Eric Mercury that drummer Jack DeJohnette had heard and when asked by Miles, did he know any electric bass players, Jack responded, yeah, I heard Harvey Brooks on this Eric Mercury album, and he was great.

…… **Bassline: *Miles Runs the Voodoo Down***

Miles Runs the Voodoo Down

Miles Davis

Seals & Crofts

I had first met and recorded with Jimmy Seals and Dash Crofts on their *Down-Home* album produced by John Simon. They liked what I played, and we connected as people. A couple of years later when working with my band the Fabulous Rhinestones in Woodstock, New York I got a call from producer Louis Shelton saying that Jimmy and Dash wanted me to come to Hollywood, Los Angeles to record. When they first played me Summer Breeze I just sat back, closed my eyes, and listened. The chord changes, harmonies, words, and music sounded so good. All it needed was a bass…. They left the bass line up to me. I had changed my La Bella flat wound strings two days before the session, so I had a bright but punchy bottom sound that only new flat wounds have.

I got to play with three of my favorite drummers at this session. Jim Keltner, Jim Gordon and John Guerin.

Bassline: *Summer Breeze*
Fender Bass
La Bella Medium Flat wound Strings
Acoustic Bass Amp

Summer Breeze

Seals & Crofts

Eric Clapton / Cream

I'm in the resort town of Sausalito, which is first exit over the Golden Gate Bridge, north of San Francisco, skimming rocks into Richardson's Bay standing alongside Cream guitarist and vocalist Eric Clapton. We had both ended up at the Trident restaurant having lunch following the opening night of a five-night gig at the Filmore Auditorium, August Twenty Ninth – September 3. I had previously met Eric at a Murray the "K" show at the RKO Theatre in New York City that was Eric's first USA concert. In San Francisco, Cream and my band, the Electric Flag were sharing the bill with Jazz vibraphonist Gary Burton whose fabulous guitarist Larry Coryell, whom I knew from jam sessions at the Café Au Go Go in Greenwich Village, New York City. The day after the opening night Bloomfield invited Larry over to the band house. It was nice to hear two masters of their own guitar styles talk about their likes and dislikes of guitar playing. Larry tried to show Michael some different chords that could be used in a blues tune, but Michael would have none of it. His mentor was B.B. King. The irony of the conversation was that the new Electric Flag featured three chord Blues tunes along with some original R&B pop tunes that drew from Otis Redding

As the Flag's bass player, I enjoyed playing the Blues tunes but some of other tunes like *Groovin' is Easy* and *Another Country*, added some additional musical color. The Electric Flag was my first band project and my first horn band experience. I learned a lot from bassist Duck Dunn of Booker T and the MG's band and the album *B.B King, Live at the Regal*

We got to talking about Mike Bloomfield and Jimi Hendrix's guitar playing styles since I had played bass with both. We drifted over to the edge of the water while talking and rock skimming into the bay. I said, Jimi Hendrix had mastered the melodic use of electronic feedback and modal chord grooves. Playing with Jimi was like getting connected to a harmonic flow of electrons that had no end. At a jam at the Café Au Go Go Jimi said, "Hey man, I got this progression, check it out". I remember jamming with him playing what was to become *Little Wing*. Jimi and I played eyeball to eyeball at many Jam sessions, clubs and concert halls. We were always in the flow of the music that fueled our spaceship. Jimi's more fluid style comes from the flashy T Bone Walker style. Jimi has more popular appeal than Bloomfield because, like T Bone, he was a showman as well as an innovator.

Michael Bloomfield / Electric Flag

I met the former Paul Butterfield blues band guitarist at the *Highway 61 Revisited* Dylan sessions in 1965. Having connected musically at the session, a few weeks later he invited me to join his new six-piece band eventually named The Electric Flag based in Mill Valley CA. The models for the band were James Brown, Otis Redding, B.B King and John Coltrane filtered through the Chicago style three chord blues. Michael was a ferocious blues traditionalist who taught me the basic Blues bass lines for his band and songs such as blues classic Howlin' Wolf's *Killing Floor.* The band created original music and rearrangements influenced by its heroes. My job with Michael was to hold down the bottom and create space for Michael and vocalist Nick Gravenites. The Electric Flag was the first pop group in the major Rock Concerts circuit of the Nineteen Seventies to bring the horn section into the frontline.

...Bassline: Killing Floor

Killing Floor
As recorded with The Electric Flag

Howlin' Wolf

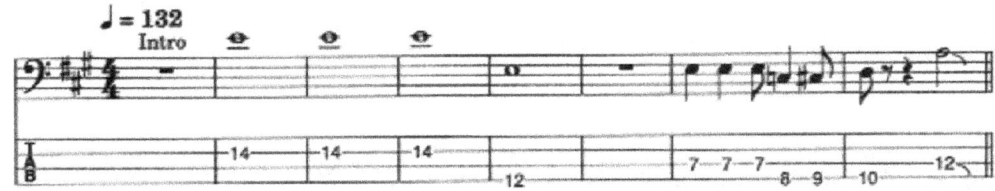

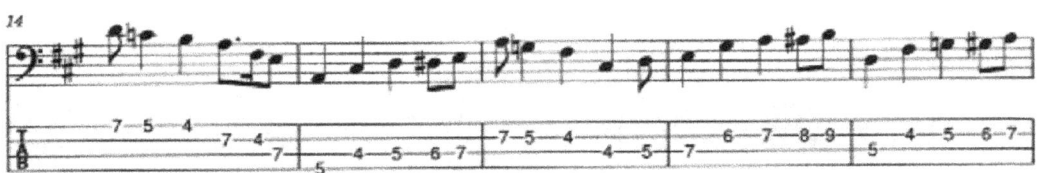

Harvey's Tune
– Super Session - In 1964 I was playing at the Ashgrove in Santa Monica CA with folksingers Jim and Jean and living in Malibu at Jean Ray's mother's house. One afternoon while sitting on the veranda facing the Pacific Ocean with the saltwater breezes filling the air, I started playing some chords and singing a melody. Over the next three or four years I kept playing the chords and singing the melody for no reason. I just liked it. I met Jean's brother Brian there. I think he must have been ten years old and had just started playing the guitar. The next time I heard about him he was the blonde-haired kid playing guitar for Etta James and the next time, with Paul McCartney.

In Nineteen Sixty-Eight I got a call from my buddy, Columbia records producer Al Kooper, to play on a project he was producing called *Super Session*. We recorded for two days. At the end of the second day Kooper said we need one more tune to finish the album. I put my bass down, borrowed Steve Stills' guitar and played the chords and sang the melody to *Harvey's Tune*. Kooper liked it. When mixing the album in New York Al added a soulful horn arrangement with Joe Scott who also added a soulful sax solo.

Bassline: Harvey's Tune
Fender Bass
La Bella Medium Flat wound Strings
Fender Dual Showman Amp

Harvey's Tune

Harvey Brooks

VARIOUS BLUES PROGRESSIONS

F7	F7	F7	F7	Bb7	Bb7	F7	F7	C7	C7	F7	F7
F7	F7	F7	F7	Bb7	Bb7	F7	F7	C7	Bb7	F7	F7
F7	Bb7	F7	F7	Bb7	Bb7	F7	F7	G7	C7	F7	C7
F7	Bb7	F7	F7	Bb7	Bb7	F7	D7	G7	C7	F7	C7
F7	Bb7	F7	F7	Bb7	Bb7	F7	D7	G-	C7	F7	G- C7
F7	Bb7	F7	C-7 F7	Bb7	Bb7	F7	A-7 D7	G-	C7	A-7 D7	G- C7
F7	Bb7	F7	C-7 F7	Bb7	Bb7	A-	D7	G-	C7	A-7 D7	G-7 C7
F7	Bb7	F7	C-7 F7	Bb7	E7b9	F7 E7	Eb7 D7	G-	C7 Bb7	A-7 D7	G-7 C7
F	E-7b5 A7	D- G7	C- F7	Bb7	B-7b5	A-	D7	G- C7	Db- Gb7	F7 D7+	G- C7+
F	Bb7	A- G-	Gb- B7	Bb7	Bb-	A-	Ab-	G-	C7+9	A-7b5 D7	G- C7+
F	Bb7	A- G-	Gb- B7	Bb7	Bb- Eb7	Ab	Ab- Db7	Gb	G- C7	A- D7	Db Gb7
F	E-7b5 A7	D- G7	C- F7	Bb	Bb- Eb7	A-	Ab- Db7	G- C7	Db Gb7	A- D7	G- C7
F#-7 B7	E- A7	D- G7	C-F7	Bb	Bb- Eb7	Ab	Ab- Db7	G-	G- C7	A-7b5 D7	G- C7
F	E-7b5 A7	D- G7	Gb- B7	Bb7	B-7b5 E7	A-	Ab- Db7	G-	C7 Bb7	A- D7	G- C7

Bass player – 12 bar blues

To begin with, each box on the chart is in 4/4 time. Your job is to just play the roots (Key note) of each chord. Either play one bar(4 quarter note plucks) or One bar with two half note plucks as they appear in each box.

Trials and Tribulations

Hollywood to Detroit Michigan

The Dylan band that played the concerts at the Forest Hills Tennis Stadium in New York City and the Hollywood Bowl in Hollywood, California featured Levon Helm on drums, Al Kooper on keyboards, Robbie Robertson on guitar and me on bass. The occasion was the unveiling of Bob Dylan's new *Highway 61 Revisited* album which was greeted by the furious folkies at Forest Hills with cheers for Dylan's acoustic set and cursing with strange noises and stage attacks for the electric set. Hollywood was totally different. Movie stars, pop music stars with glam and glitter. Dylan's whole show was accepted and was the talk of the town.

Now I'm anxious to see what's next. The only thing is that I have a three-week gig in Detroit. So, I call Dylan's office and tell them I'm out of town for three weeks and that I'll check in. I could have subbed out the gig (get someone else to do the Detroit gig) but I felt obligated to fulfill my verbal contract.

So, I'm playing in a Trini Lopez type trio and living in a no window hotel in Cadillac Square, Detroit Michigan, checking in on the next Dylan tour by phone. While I'm checking in, the rest of Levon and the Hawks had checked me out. While the iron is hot you can change the shape, add or takeaway. Once the iron cools down, whatever is done is done. While I was in Detroit, Mary Martin, working for Dylan's manager Albert Grossman, had heard the Hawks in Toronto, Canada. Dylan was being directed in the heat of the moment to Toronto Canada to hear the rest of Levon and Robbie's band, the Hawks. The rest is history. If you don't know it, look it up in my book "View from the Bottom."

Producer – Studio Manager

I had been hired to go to Atlanta Georgia in 1976 to play on singer/songwriter Robert Lee's album at Axis Sound Studio in Atlanta Georgia. After the project was finished, I was offered the job of co-studio manager to help bring in business using my name and credits. In my mind, since disco music had eliminated most electric bass guitar from the studio, being replaced by keyboard bass lines, and my band the Fabulous Rhinestones breaking up, I took the job. We did a lot of quality music. Bassist Duck Dunn, bass player with Booker 'T' and the MGs, and producer Jeff Glixman, with the group Kansas, were some of the projects as well as St. Louis born Keyboardist and co-studio manager Bill King and Gospel singer Jeremy Olds.

This Bud's For You

One day I was in the studio listening to some mixes when the front desk calls me and says a guy named Lonnie Mack is here and wants to meet me. Now Lonnie Mack had a huge instrumental hit with the Chuck Berry song *Memphis*. He was a powerful guitar player and singer, and I had no idea why he was here. I came out of the studio, and he said, "I heard a lot about you and thought I'd come over and check you out". I'm figuring he wants to check out the studio. We go back into the studio and he's checking out the control room and we eventually gravitate to the piano which is in the center of the studio and has a spotlight on it left over from a previous gospel session and we sat down and talked. He starts telling me about this new group he just joined. He and this guy Ed Labunsky, who was a commercial jingle writer, was building a recording studio in Milford PA, and was putting together a country and western band called South and would I be interested in joining up with them. Ed's most famous jingle was ......*This Bud's for You*, a Budweiser beer commercial that made him millions and financed his new project.

After two years at Axis Sound, even with the excellent weed, the studio became routine, and I was missing the excitement of the live gig and the insanity of Rock 'N' Roll. The project sounded weird and wacky, so I accepted Lonnie's invitation. Packed up my Chevy Van and with the help of my dad, Sam Goldstein, who flew down from New York City, Queens Village to keep me company. Father and Son left Axis Sound Studio and Atlanta GA two weeks later and headed for Milford PA. Pop was a retired long haul truck driver and was excited about riding in the navigator's seat enjoying the scenery instead of being the driver. We bonded on that trip. He smoked his first joint. It was a meeting of the generations. We camped one night in a Blue Ridge Mountain camp site and settled some father and son misunderstandings between us as we watched shooting stars in the night sky. I dropped Pop off in Queens, went upstairs for a cup of coffee and a hug with mom, then hit the road heading for Milford, Pennsylvania.

Back to Ed Labunsky and South

My brother Gary and family moved down to help build the studio and Gary was the recording engineer as well as playing saxophone and bass. It was like Camp South for songwriters. Each band member had his own room. There were portable cassette players, pads and pencils at every chair, a fridge full of beer and a bar full of whiskey. In the kitchen there was a long French farm table that I thought was specifically for meals. Many an acey deucy card game was played on that table and hundreds of dollars were won and lost on every hand. The music had only just begun when Labunsky had a fatal car accident on the way to the studio. All that work to build his studio and create the music he loved was over. Shortly after, I joined Clarence Clemons Red Bank Rockers.

Playing with The Big Man

Bruce Springsteen's Big Man, Clarence Clemons, had a big band, The Red Bank Rockers. Five horns, trumpet, trombone, tenor, baritone, and Clarence on alto sax. The band was based in Red Bank NJ at Clarence's nightclub named "Big Man's West". Since most of the tunes we played were either Stax or Motown cover tunes and on occasion playing some Bruce Springsteen tunes such as *Fire* with Springsteen jamming with us. The job for me was to connect the rhythm section (guitar, bass, drums and keyboards) to the horn section by locking in with the drummer's bass drum pattern and hi-hat feel. Since there was so much good music going on stage, my basslines had to be simple. Doubling the horn licks or guitar rhythm hits and creating my own bassline melodies with the horn section. Clarence was a great guy, with a good sense of humor and didn't allow any substance abusers on his stage. He ran the band with his own set of rules.

Chapter Eight

Reading Music

I started guitar lessons with guitar teacher Jerry Oddo. I learned some basics and enjoyed his lessons. He made playing the guitar fun, as I wrote in my book, "View from the Bottom" published by Tangible Press.

Guitar lessons were the extent of my formal musical education. While continuing guitar I started lessons on the tenor saxophone at Martin Van Buren high school. After two weeks of saxophone, the band's music director walked into the classroom and pulled me out of the class saying you are just the right size to play double Bb sousaphone giving me my first experience with the bass clef. Shortly after starting my sousaphone lessons, I joined a band named The Citations as the second guitar player. The Citations acquired a manager who suggested that since we had two guitar players, I should replace my second guitar with a bass guitar.

In my senior year, while my High School music training was going on, with the support of my parents' car, I was going over the Williamsburg Bridge into Manhattan's Greenwich Village playing bass at the dance clubs and music bars. After my Martin Van Buren High School Orchestra career as a sousaphone player ended when the Eastman School of Music rejected me, my four to six nights of playing electric bass every week paid off. Playing the gigs I was playing, I didn't need to read music notes. It wasn't required. Reading chord charts was sufficient. I was nineteen years old and making a living.

It wasn't until I started doing recording sessions that reading music became a requirement. There are many financial opportunities that become available to a musician who can read music. When your regular pop band is rehearsing for its first gig or a new album, you still got to eat. You can fill in for a bass player who's double booked, or you can get to be known in the commercial or session world as a guy who's a good reader and a quick learner. The fact that you can sit down with a sheet of music and be part of a musical experience quickly and energetically, is another tool in your arsenal.

MUSICAL SYMBOLS

Music consists of two basic elements: **rhythm** and **pitch**. Pitch is notated using a set of lines (and spaces) called a staff. The higher a note appears on a staff, the higher its pitch; the lower a note appears, the lower its pitch. At the beginning of the staff is a clef sign. Bass music is written in the bass clef or "F clef."

STAFF **BASS CLEF**

The two dots in the clef sign surround the line on which the pitch "F" is written; hence the term "F clef."

The musical alphabet uses the letters **A**, **B**, **C**, **D**, **E**, **F**, and **G**. After G, the sequence repeats starting with A. In bass clef, the notes written on the **lines** of the staff are G–B–D–F–A. You can remember this sequence as "Good Boys Do Fine Always." The notes on the **spaces** are A–C–E–G. "All Cows Eat Grass" may help you remember this.

LINES G B D F A   **SPACES** A C E G

Rhythm, the other basic element of music, is notated using **measures** (also known as "bars"), which contain a set number of beats (the pulse of the music). Each measure is separated from the next by a **bar line**. A double bar line is used to show the end of a section of music. The final bar line is used to show the end of a piece of music.

MEASURE   MEASURE
BAR LINE   BAR LINE   DOUBLE BAR LINE (end of section)   FINAL BAR LINE (end of song)

The number of beats in each measure is indicated by the **time signature**, which appears at the start of a piece after the clef sign. The time signature looks like a fraction. The top number tells us how many beats there are in a bar, and the bottom number tells us what type of note is to be counted. Most of the examples in this book will be in 4/4 time.

TIME SIGNATURE → four beats per measure
→ a quarter note (♩) gets one beat

In the first part of this book, you will see three different kinds of note values. They are:

NOTE VALUES

QUARTER NOTE = 1 beat   HALF NOTE = 2 beats   WHOLE NOTE = 4 beats

THE RHYTHMIC ALPHABET PT. 2

These are **ALL** of the sixteenth note figures of the Rhythmic Alphabet.
Practice each one of these separately, one each day, for 30 days.

Road Map

𝄆 𝄇   Repeat Enclosures – Play everything in between the repeat signs <u>twice</u>, unless more repeats (3x) are indicated.

A   Section marker – The A section is usually a verse.

⊕   Coda – The first one is an EXIT point, the one at the bottom is the ENTRY point to the end of the song.

Tag   The street term for "Coda" it means repeat the <u>last phrase</u> (sometimes more than once), then play the ending.

𝄋   "Del Segno" means 'the sign" – Marks the re-entry point into the form; a double-back point.

D.C. al coda   "Del Capo" means go to "the top", or the very beginning of the song, then jump to the coda (ending).

D.S. al Coda   "Del Segno" means double back to the SIGN, then jump to the coda (ending).

1.   First ending sign – play the measures under the bracket and then double back to the repeat sign.

2.   Second ending sign – play the measures under the bracket and then double back to the repeat sign, or continue on through the form.

Fine   Means "THE END"!

GROOVE MECHANICS

Steps to Building a Solid Groove

1. **JUST PLAY THE ROOTS!**
   - Lock in with the Kick drum
   - This is your basic groove pattern; you only ADD to it

2. **ADD IN ½ STEP APPROACH TONES.**
   - is your basic groove pattern; you only ADD to it

3. **ADD THE 5TH AND THE OCTAVE.**
   - Keep the same groove pattern going at all times

4. **BUILD A "RIFF" USING THE CHORD TONES.**
   - Always keep your basic groove pattern going!
   - Move the riff from chord to chord with the changes

5. **USE A CONNECTING LINE FROM ROOT TO ROOT.**
   - Just think about going UP or DOWN to connect to the next root

6. **ADD "FILLS" BETWEEN EACH SECTION OF THE SONG.**
   - Use chord tones in any sequence
   - Use a triplet rhythm to create a rhythmic variation

© Lynne Davis-Witten 2004

Afterword

"I have been playing, recording, studying and moving to the music, all my life. The music keeps me in touch with who, what and where. I keep my ears open for that tune that makes me pull off the road to hear it again. Be who you are. My job as a bass player is to lay down a solid groove for everyone to lock in to. I always lock with the drummer. The drummer is a bass player's best friend. He creates the world of time that signals the other players to the path to follow"

I'm eighty years old and fortunate enough to have grown up in a time when recorded music began to reach all segments of society. Lots of places for musicians to play. Multi-act concert shows put on by disc jockeys like Alan Freed and Murry the K exposed American audiences to Rock 'N' Roll and R&B (Rhythm & Blues). Music clubs, coffee houses for listening, dancing, and hanging out. It was a humbler time. Entertainment was affordable and artists became popular based on their hit songs and personality. Because of this environment musicians had the opportunity to hone their skills by playing different styles of music and artists began to write their own songs and lyrics.

I missed out on learning and getting a classical music education. I suggest all musicians get as much education as possible. It greatly enhances your ability to make a living and increases your ability to musically communicate with all styles of music.

My education, came from Jazz lounge bands, R&B and Pop top ten gigs. I listened to Motown records bassist James Jameson, Stax records Duck Dunn, Atlantic records Chuck Rainey, Beatles Paul McCartney and James Brown Bootsy Collins, B.B. King and the Rolling Stones, Steely Dan and the Eagles. Whatever your era or taste in music is, listen and learn the bass line and the chord progression.

There are many great books and videos available to help you learn about playing the electric bass. I recommend Ed Friedland's 'Bass Method" and Lynne-Davis Witten for the use of her lesson sheets. Achieving the skills using scales and ear training exercises help you to hear the bassline of a song and by using the repetition method of singing the line over and over, then playing it on the bass allows you to hear and visualize the key and tone center. Playing music with other musicians in my opinion is the best music school you can study in. Always try to play with musicians who are equal or better than you and have had more experience.

> *"Music begins where the possibilities of Language end."*
>
> **Jean Sibelius**

My Favorite Bass Players

Charlie Mingus
Scott LaFaro
Ron Carter
Paul Chambers
Dave Holland
Chuck Rainey
Jaco Pastorius
Steve Swallow
Willie Dixon
Duck Dunn
Tony Levin
Jerry Jammott
James Jamerson
Rocco Prestia
Bob Moore
Rick Danko
Charlie Haden
Larry Graham
Paul McCartney
Carol Kaye
Bootsy Collins
Bob Babbit

Appendix

Harvey Brooks – Discography

1. Bob Dylan – *Highway 61 Revisited* – Columbia – 1965

    a. Single – "*Positively 4th Street*"

2. Tom Rush – *Take a Little Walk with Me* – Elektra – 1966

3. Eric Andersen – *That's Alright Mama* – Vanguard – 1966

4. David Blue – *David Blue* – Elektra – 1966

5. Jim & Jean – *Changes* – Verve Folkways – 1966

6. Harvey Brooks – *How to Play Electric Bass* – Elektra – 1967

7. The Electric Flag – *The Trip: Original Motion Picture Soundtrack* – Sidewalk – 1967

8. Ian & Sylvia – *Lovin' Sound* – MGM – 1967

9. Peter, Paul and Mary – *Album 1700* – Warner Bros. – 1967

    a. Single: "*I Dig Rock and Roll Music*"

10. Eric Andersen – *'Bout Changes 'N Things* – Vanguard – 1967

11. Mike Bloomfield, Stephen Stills, Al Kooper – *Super Session* – Columbia – 1968

12. Richie Havens – *Mixed Bag* – Verve Forecast – 1968

13. Mama Cass – *Dream a Little Dream* – ABC/Dunhill – 1968

14. The Electric Flag – *A Long Time Comin'* – Columbia – 1968

15. The Electric Flag – *An American Music Band* – Columbia – 1968

16. Freakout – *You Are What You Eat (Original Soundtrack)* – Columbia Masterworks – 1968

17. Hedge and Donna – *All the Friendly Colours* – Capitol Records – 1969

18. Eric Mercury – *Electric Black Man* – AVCO Embassy – 1969

19. Sonuvagun – *Last Summer (Original Motion Picture Soundtrack)* – Warner Bros./Seven Arts – 1969

20. The Doors – *The Soft Parade* – Elektra – 1969

    a. Singles – "Touch Me," "Wishful Sinful," "Tell All the People"

21. Tony Kosinec – *Processes* – Columbia – 1969

22. Karen Dalton – *So Hard to Tell Who's Going to Love You the Best* – Capitol Records – 1969

23. Kathy McCord – *Kathy McCord* – CTI Records – 1970

24. John and Beverley Martyn – *Stormbringer* – Island Records – 1970

25. John Sebastian – *John B. Sebastian* – Reprise – 1970

26. Starship – Paul Kantner – *Blows Against the Empire* – RCA Victor – 1970

27. Miles Davis – *Bitches Brew* – Columbia – 1970

28. Bob Dylan – *New Morning* – Columbia – 1970

    a. Single – "*If Not for You*"

29. John Cale – *Vintage Violence* – Columbia – 1970

30. Bobby Lester – *Bobby Lester* – Columbia – 1970

31. Seals and Crofts – *Down Home* – T-A Records – 1970

32. John Hall – *Action* – Columbia – 1970

33. Al Kooper – *Brand New Day – Landlords soundtrack* – Columbia Records – 1971

34. John Simon – *John Simon's Album* – Warner Bros. – 1971

35. Pacheco and Alexander – *Pacheco and Alexander* – Columbia – 1971

36. Seals and Crofts – *Summer Breeze* – Warner Bros. – 1971

    a. Singles: "*Summer Breeze*" and "*Hummingbird*"

37. Fabulous Rhinestones – *The Fabulous Rhinestones* – Just Sunshine Records – 1972

38. Fabulous Rhinestones – *Freewheelin* – Just Sunshine Records – 1973

39. John Compton – *To Luna* – Ageless Records – 1973

40. Rosalie Sorrels – *Whatever Happened to the Girl That Was* – Paramount Records – 1973

41. Rachel Faro – *Refugees* – RCA Victor – 1974

42. Miles Davis – *Big Fun* – Columbia – 1974

43. The Rhinestones – *The Rhinestones* – 20th Century Records – 1975

44. Loudon Wainwright III – *Unrequited* – CBS – 1975

45. Al Kooper – *Anthology/Al's Big Deal/Unclaimed Freight* – Columbia – 1975

46. Gilles Rivard – *Impulsions* – Sonogram – 1975

47. Leo's Sunship – *We Need Each Other* – Lyons Record Co. Inc. – 1978

48. Miles Davis – *Circle in the Round* – Columbia – 1979

49. Tony Wilson – *Catch One* – Bearsville – 1979

50. Jerome Olds – *You Lift Me Up* – Heartstring – 1980

51. Miles Davis – *Un Enigma Da Musica Negro-Americana* – Abril Cultural – 1980

52. The Doors – Greatest Hits – Elektra – 1980

53. Michael Bloomfield – *Bloomfield: A Retrospective* – Columbia – 1983

54. Electric Flag – *The Best of the Electric Flag* – Back-Trac Records, CBS Special Products – 1984

55. Miles Davis – *A Portrait of Miles Davis* – CBS – 1987

56. Jimi Hendrix – *Café Au Go Go Jam Session* – Koiné Records 1988

57. Jimi Hendrix – *Jammin' with Friends* – Koiné Records – 1989

58. Miles Davis – *The Columbia Years 1955-1985* – Columbia – 1988

59. Miles Davis – *Volume 3* – Columbia – 1981

60. Bob Dylan – *The Bootleg Series Volumes 1-3 (Rare & Unreleased)* 1961-1991 – Columbia – 1991

61. John Sebastian – *Tar Beach* – Shanachie Records – 1992

62. Neal Black and the Healers – *Neal Black and the Healers* – Dixie Frog – 1993

63. Al Kooper – *Rekooperation* – Music Masters – 1994

64. Michael Bloomfield – *Don't Say That I Ain't Your Man!* – Essential Blues 1964-1969 – Legacy, Col. – 1994

65. John Cale – *Seducing Down the Door* – A Collection 1970 – 1990 – Rhino – 1994

66. Miles Davis – *Le Meilleur De Miles Davis* – Columbia – 1994

67. The Fabulous Thunderbirds – *Roll of the Dice* – Private Music – 1995

68. Fontella Bass – *No Ways Tired* – Nonsuch – 1995

69. John Simon – *Harmony Farm* – Pioneer – 1995

70. Peter Green Songbook – *Viceroy Music Europe* – 1995

71. Al Kooper – *Soul of a Man* – Music Masters – 1995

72. Groovy: A Collection of Rare Jazzy Club Tracks – 1996

73. Bob Dylan – *The Best of Bob Dylan* – Sony Music TV/Columbia – 1997

74. Paul Burlison – *Train Kept a-Rollin'* – Sweetish Records – 1997

75. Miles Davis – *The Complete Bitches Brew Sessions* – Columbia Legacy – 1998

76. Bob Dylan – *From Newport to the Ancient Empty Street in LA* – Dandelion – 1998

77. Tom Rush – *The Very Best of Tom Rush* – Columbia Legacy/Common Chord – 1999

78. The Doors – *The Complete Studio Recordings* – Elektra – 1999

79. Paul Pena – *New Train* – Hybrid Recordings – 2000

80. Ken Burns Jazz – *The Story of America's Music* – Columbia Legacy – 2000

81. Miles Davis – *The Essential Miles Davis* – Columbia Legacy – 2001

82. Raisins in the Sun – *Raisins in the Sun* – Rounder – 2001

83. Miles Davis – *The Best of Miles Davis* – Columbia Legacy – 2002

84. Bob Dylan – *No Direction Home: The Soundtrack* – Columbia Classic Records – 2005

85. Various Artists: *Sous Les Paves, LeJazz* – Sony BMG Music/Columbia Legacy – 2008

86. Various Artists: *The All New Electric Muse Album* – Universal Music/Operations Limited – 2008

87. The 17th Street Band – *Positively 17th Street* – 17th Street Records – 2009

88. Francisco Gonzalez – *The Gift* – 17th Street Records – 2009

89. Bob Dylan – *The Original Mono Recordings* – Columbia – 2010

90. Richie Havens – *Mixed Bag/Something Else Again* – Raven Records – 2010

91. The Doors – *A Collection (6-CD Set)* – Elektra/Rhino Records – Doors Music Co. – 2011

92. Rob Paparozzi – *The Ed Palermo Big Band* – Electric Butter – 2014

93. Bob Dylan – *Bob Dylan's 50th Anniversary Collection 1965* – Columbia Legacy – 2015

94. Bob Dylan – *The Best of the Cutting Edge 1965-1966* – Columbia Legacy – 2015

95. The Electric Flag – *The Electric Flag Featuring Erma Franklin/Live 1968* – Rockbeat Records – 2015

96. Betty Davis – *The Columbia Years 1968-69* – Light in the Attic –2016

97. Harvey Brooks -*Elegant Geezer / Jerusalem Sessions* – Elegant Geezer Records - 2021

Thank You:

Bonnie Brooks

A.J. Wachtel

Dan Naiman

Frank Beacham

Larry Hartke – https://www.hartke.com/artists/harvey-brooks/

Richard Coco- https://www.labella.com/artists/harvey-brooks/

Chris Larsen & Sally Larsen– Cover design

Doug & Jen Bartlett

John Howells – Book design and Publisher

Extra bass information

Bass guitar strings are composed of a core and winding. The core is a wire which runs through the center of the string and is made of steel, nickel, or an [alloy](#).[9] The winding is a smaller gauge wire wrapped around the core. Bass guitar strings vary by the material and cross-sectional shape of the winding.

Common string variants include roundwound, flatwound, halfwound (groundwound), coated, tapewound and taperwound strings. Roundwound and flatwound strings feature windings with circular and rounded-square cross-sections, respectively, with half-round strings being a hybrid between the two. Coated strings have their surface coated with a synthetic layer while tapewound strings feature a metal core with a plastic winding.[10][11][12] Taperwound strings have a tapered end where the exposed core sits on the bridge saddle without windings.[13] The choice of winding has considerable impact on the sound of the instrument, with certain winding styles often being preferred for certain musical genres.[14]

In the 1950s, [Leo Fender](#) and [George Fullerton](#) developed the first mass-produced electric bass guitar.[18] The [Fender Electric Instrument Manufacturing Company](#) began producing the [Precision Bass](#), or P-Bass, in October 1951. The design featured a simple uncontoured "slab" body design (with no edge contours) and a [single coil pickup](#), both features similar to a [Telecaster](#). By 1957, the Precision Bass began to resemble the [Fender Stratocaster](#) with the body edges beveled for comfort and the pickup changed to a separate halves [split coil](#) design.[19]

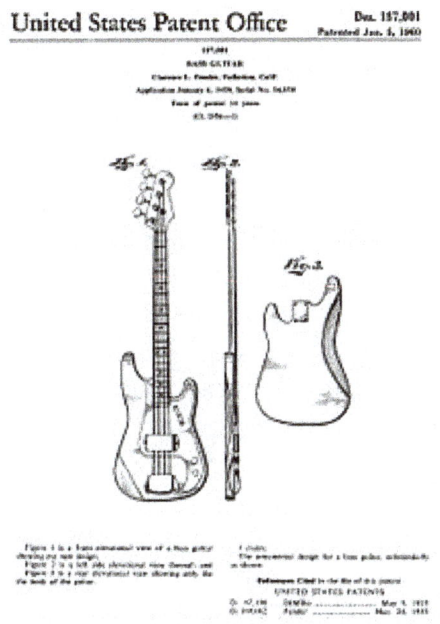

Design patent issued to Leo Fender for the second-generation Precision Bass

The Fender Bass was a revolutionary instrument for working musicians. In comparison to the upright bass, the bass guitar could be easily transported. When amplified, the bass guitar was also much less prone than acoustic basses to audio feedback.[20] The addition of frets enabled bassists to play in tune more easily than on upright basses, and allowed guitarists to more easily play the instrument.[21]

In 1953, Monk Montgomery became the first bassist to tour with the Fender bass, in Lionel Hampton's postwar big band.[22][23] Montgomery was also possibly the first to record with the electric bass, on July 2, 1953, with the Art Farmer Septet.[24] Roy Johnson (with Lionel Hampton), and Shifty Henry (with Louis Jordan and His Tympany Five), were other early Fender bass pioneers.[18] Bill Black, who played with Elvis Presley and James Jamerson switched from upright bass to the Fender Precision Bass around 1957.[25] The bass guitar was intended to appeal to guitarists as well as upright bass players, and many early pioneers of the instrument, such as Joe Osborn, and Paul McCartney were originally guitarists.[20]

https://en.wikipedia.org/wiki/List_of_bass_guitar_manufacturers

Bass bodies are typically made of wood although other materials such as graphite (for example, some of the Steinberger designs) have also been used. While a wide variety of woods are suitable for use in the body, neck, and fretboard of the bass guitar – the most common type of wood used for the body is alder, for the neck is maple, and for the fretboard is rosewood. Other commonly used woods include mahogany, maple, ash, and poplar for bodies, mahogany for necks, and ebony for fretboards.

Bass guitar necks, which are longer than regular electric guitar necks, are generally made of maple. More exotic woods include bubinga, wenge, ovangkol, ebony and goncalo alves. Graphite or carbon fiber are used to make lightweight necks[11] and, in some cases, entire basses.[12]

Exotic woods are used on more expensive instruments: for example, the company 'Alembic' is associated with the use of cocobolo as a body material or top layer because of its attractive grain. Warwick bass guitars are also well-known for exotic hardwoods: most of the necks are made of ovangkol, and the fingerboards wenge or ebony. Solid bubinga bodies are also used for tonic and aesthetic qualities.

The "long scale" necks used on Leo Fender's basses, giving a scale length (distance between nut and bridge) of 34", remain the standard for electric basses. However, 30" or "short scale" instruments, such as the Höfner Violin Bass, played by Paul McCartney, and the Fender Mustang Bass are popular, especially for players with smaller hands. While 35", 35.5" and 36" scale lengths were once only available in "boutique" instruments, in the 2000s, many manufacturers have begun offering these lengths, also called an "extra long scale." This extra long scale provides a higher string tension, which yields a more defined tone on the low "B" string of 5- and 6-stringed instruments (or detuned 4-string basses).

Fretted and fretless basses

Another design consideration for the bass is whether to use frets on the fingerboard. On a fretted bass, the frets divide the fingerboard into semitone divisions (as on a normal guitar). The original Fender basses had 20 frets, but modern basses may have 24 or more.

Fretless basses have a distinct sound, because the absence of frets means that the string must be pressed down directly onto the wood of the fingerboard. The string buzzes against the wood, as with the double bass, creating a "mwaah" sound. The fretless bass allows players to use the expressive devices of glissando, vibrato and microtonal intonations such as quarter tones and just intonation. Some bassists use both fretted and fretless basses in performances, according to the type of material they are performing. While fretless basses are often associated with jazz and jazz fusion, bassists from other genres use fretless basses, such as metal bassist Steve DiGiorgio. The first fretless bass guitar was made by Bill Wyman in 1961 when he converted an inexpensive Japanese fretted bass by removing the frets. [13][14] The first production fretless bass was the Ampeg AUB-1 introduced in 1966, and Fender introduced a fretless Precision Bass in 1970. In the early 1970s, fusion-jazz bassist Jaco Pastorius created his own fretless bass by removing the frets[15] from a Fender Jazz Bass, filling the holes with wood putty, and coating the fretboard with epoxy resin.[16]

Some fretless basses have "fret line" markers inlaid in the fingerboard as a guide, while others only use guide marks on the side of the neck. Tapewound (Double Bass Type) strings are sometimes used with the fretless bass so that the metal string windings will not wear down the fingerboard. Some fretless basses have fingerboards which are coated with epoxy to increase the durability of the fingerboard, enhance sustain and give a brighter tone. Although most fretless basses have four strings, five-string and six-string fretless basses are also available. Fretless basses with more than six strings are also available as "boutique" or custom-made instruments.

www.ingramcontent.com/pod-product-compliance
Lightning Source LLC
LaVergne TN
LVHW061346060426
835512LV00012B/2585